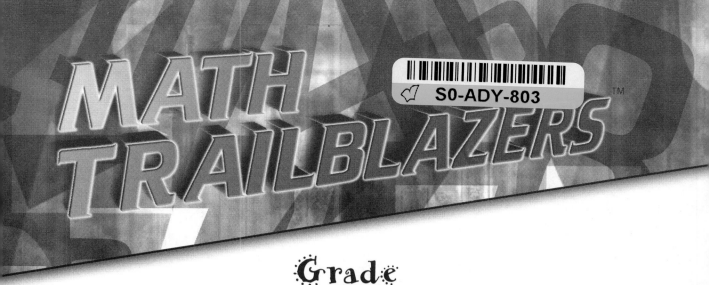

MATH TRAILBLAZERS™

Grade
2

Unit Resource Guide
Unit 8
Multiple Masses

SECOND EDITION

A Mathematical Journey Using Science and Language Arts

KENDALL/HUNT PUBLISHING COMPANY
4050 Westmark Drive   Dubuque, Iowa 52002

A TIMS® Curriculum
University of Illinois at Chicago

UIC The University of Illinois
at Chicago

The original edition was based on work supported by the National Science Foundation under grant No. MDR 9050226 and the University of Illinois at Chicago. Any opinions, findings, and conclusions or recommendations expressed in this publication are those of the author(s) and do not necessarily reflect the views of the granting agencies.

LETTER HOME

Multiple Masses

Date: _____

Dear Family Member:

We often use the terms "weight" and "mass" interchangeably, but technically, they are not the same. Mass is the amount of matter in an object. Weight is the pull of gravity on that object. Your child will learn about mass and weight in this unit.

We will use an equal-arm balance to measure the mass of everyday objects, record findings on a data table, and then graph the data. When we analyze the data as a class, we'll see that an object's material is an important factor to consider when thinking about the mass of an object.

You can provide additional support at home.

I just found out that my shoe's mass is 280 grams.

Using an equal-arm balance to find the mass of a shoe

- **Bagging Produce.** When you are at the grocery store, let your child help select and bag fruits and vegetables. Ask your child to estimate the weight of each bag and then find the weight using a scale.

- **Ordering Masses.** At home, ask your child to arrange several packaged food items in order by mass. The net weight and mass are usually written on the package in ounces and grams. Help your child read the labels to confirm that the packages are placed in the correct order. Does a small item ever have a greater mass than a large item? Is your child surprised by this? Discuss why this happens.

- **Addition Facts.** We are now studying the addition facts in Group F (9 + 1, 9 + 2, 9 + 3, 9 + 4, 10 + 1, 10 + 2, 10 + 3, 10 + 4). Help your child learn these facts by using the *Triangle Flash Cards.*

Thank you for your continued support in making math a part of your child's everyday life.

Sincerely,

_____

UNIT OUTLINE

Multiple Masses
Pacing Suggestions

Each of the lessons in this unit explores mass. Make use of the connections to science and language arts that are built into this unit. For example, students can collect the data for Lesson 3 during science time.

Components Key: SG = Student Guide, AB = Adventure Book, URG = Unit Resource Guide, and DPP = Daily Practice and Problems

	Sessions	Description	Supplies
LESSON 1 **Putting Masses in Order** SG pages 194–202 URG pages 14–21 DPP A–D	2	**ACTIVITY:** Students explore the concept of mass, using carefully selected objects and the equal-arm balance. **ASSESSMENT PAGE:** *Analyzing the Masses of Two Blocks,* Student Guide, page 199.	• equal-arm balances • clay • one-inch wood spheres • one-inch glass spheres • half-inch steel spheres • connecting cubes • envelopes
LESSON 2 **The Mouse-Proof Shelf** AB pages 31–44 SG pages 203–204 URG pages 22–30 DPP E–F	1	**ADVENTURE BOOK:** Students use an interactive story about four mice searching for cheese as a springboard for work with problems that have multiple solutions.	• connecting cubes • equal-arm balances

	Sessions	Description	Supplies
LESSON 3 **Measuring Mass** SG pages 205–211 URG pages 31–42 DPP G–L	3	**LAB:** Students determine the mass in grams of objects by using an equal-arm balance and a set of standard masses. They record the data on a graph and analyze the results.	• equal-arm balances • objects less than 100 grams • objects approximately 100 grams each • standard metric masses

CONNECTIONS

A current list of connections is available at www.mathtrailblazers.com.

Software

- *Discover Time* provides practice in telling time to the nearest hour, half-hour, quarter hour, and five-minute intervals.

- *Graphers* is a data-graphing tool appropriate for young students.

- *Kid Pix* helps students draw, write, and illustrate math concepts.

- *Math Concepts One . . . Two . . . Three!* estimates and measures time, money, length, temperature, and mass.

Multiple Masses

This unit has three major goals:

- to provide experiences that help students explore the concept of mass;
- to provide experiences in measuring mass or weight using equal-arm balances and standard masses (grams); and
- to provide opportunities to use repeated addition and skip counting.

The first lesson gives students experiences in zeroing the equal-arm balance and comparing the mass of objects. This lesson helps students discover that larger objects do not necessarily have more mass. For example, a ball of lead with a one-inch diameter has considerably more mass than a ball of cheese with a two-inch diameter.

The Adventure Book *The Mouse-Proof Shelf* takes a whimsical look at the results of unbalanced masses. The late-night adventures of four mice in their quest for cheese provide the opportunity to launch a multi-solution problem.

The final lesson, a laboratory investigation, introduces grams as the metric unit for mass. To find the mass of an object, students place the object in one pan of the equal-arm balance and standard masses in the other until the two pans balance. Determining the total value of the masses can be accomplished efficiently with repeated addition and skip counting.

Notes on Mass vs. Weight

In conversational speech, we talk about the weight of an object rather than its mass. These words are not synonymous. Technically, weight and mass are distinct concepts. In scientific terms, the **mass** of an object is the amount of matter in the object. In elementary grades we use an equal-arm balance to measure mass. The **weight** of an object is the measure of the pull of gravity on that object.

Children and adults usually talk about one object weighing more than another. During this unit, you will probably hear your students saying that they are "weighing" an object rather than "massing" it. It is acceptable for students to use these terms interchangeably. However, encourage your students to use the proper language for mass. For example, guide students to say that something "has a mass of 110 grams," rather than "weighs 110 grams."

Since students are already familiar with space travel, use this context to explain the difference between mass and weight. Many children know that the pull of gravity varies on different planets and that there is essentially no gravity in outer space. Tell them to imagine that they are astronauts traveling to the moon. Once they have reached their destination, they decide to check their changes in weight and mass. They discover that they weigh less on the moon, but their masses have stayed the same.

Since the moon's gravity is weaker than Earth's, the pull on an individual object is less. Therefore, students would weigh less on the moon than on Earth. In contrast, the mass of an object remains constant regardless of space travel because gravity does not influence mass. Since an equal-arm balance is used to measure mass, both sides of the scale are equally affected by gravity. For example, an 11-gram pencil balances one 1-gram and two 5-gram standard masses on Earth and it will balance those same masses on the moon.

For further information on mass, refer to the TIMS Tutor: *The Concept of Mass* in the *Teacher Implementation Guide*.

Assessment Indicators

- Can students compare the mass of objects using a balance?
- Can students measure mass in grams?
- Can students make and interpret bar graphs?
- Can students solve computation problems involving mass?
- Do students demonstrate fluency with the addition facts in Group F?

OBSERVATIONAL ASSESSMENT RECORD

(A1) Can students compare the mass of objects using a balance?

(A2) Can students measure mass in grams?

(A3) Can students make and interpret bar graphs?

(A4) Can students solve computation problems involving mass?

(A5) Do students demonstrate fluency with the addition facts in Group F?

(A6) _____

Name	A1	A2	A3	A4	A5	A6	Comments
1.							
2.							
3.							
4.							
5.							
6.							
7.							
8.							
9.							
10.							
11.							
12.							
13.							

Name	A1	A2	A3	A4	A5	A6	Comments
14.							
15.							
16.							
17.							
18.							
19.							
20.							
21.							
22.							
23.							
24.							
25.							
26.							
27.							
28.							
29.							
30.							
31.							
32.							

Daily Practice and Problems

Multiple Masses

Two Daily Practice and Problems (DPP) items are included for each class session listed in the Unit Outline. A Scope and Sequence Chart for the DPP for the year can be found in the *Teacher Implementation Guide.*

A DPP Menu for Unit 8

Icons designate the subject matter of the DPP items in the Teacher Notes column. Each item falls into one or more of the categories listed below. A brief menu of the DPP items for Unit 8 follows.

N Number Sense	Computation	Time	Geometry
C, D, F, J, L	D	B	H
Math Facts	$ Money	Measurement	Data
A, E, G–I, K	G	J, L	

Practice and Assessment of the Addition Facts

The DPP in this unit continues the yearlong strategies-based approach to practicing and assessing the addition and subtraction facts. DPP items in this unit provide review and assessment of the addition facts in Group F ($9 + 1, 9 + 2, 9 + 3, 9 + 4, 10 + 1, 10 + 2, 10 + 3, 10 + 4$). Facts in this group can be solved by using a ten and counting on. DPP item A asks students to use the *Triangle Flash Cards* to study these facts. *Triangle Flash Cards: Group F* can be found in the *Student Guide* as homework for

Lesson 1. See DPP items A, E, G, and K for practice with these facts and item I for an assessment. Use Assessment Indicator (A5) and the *Observational Assessment Record* to document students' progress with these facts.

For information on the practice and assessment of the addition and subtraction facts in Grade 2, see the DPP Guides for Units 3 and 11 and the *Grade 2 Facts Resource Guide.* For a detailed explanation of our approach to learning and assessing the facts in Grades K–5, see the TIMS Tutor: *Math Facts* in the *Teacher Implementation Guide.*

Daily Practice and Problems

Students may solve the items individually, in groups, or as a class. The items may also be assigned for homework.

Student Questions	Teacher Notes

 A *Triangle Flash Cards: Group F*

With a partner, use your *Triangle Flash Cards* to practice addition facts. Separate the cards into three piles: those facts you know and can answer quickly, those facts that you can figure out with a strategy, and those that you need to learn. Discuss the strategies that you use with your partner.

The *Triangle Flash Cards: Group F* are located in the *Student Guide* as a Homework Page for Lesson 1 and in the *Unit Resource Guide* Generic Section. Ask students to work with a partner to study the facts using the flash cards. One partner covers the corner with the largest number on the card. The second partner adds the remaining two numbers.

Repeat the process with the second partner finding the sums. Encourage students to discuss the strategies they use to solve the problems. Remind students to take their cards home to study for homework. Give students envelopes to store their cards.

Inform students when the quiz on the facts in Group F will be given. This quiz appears in DPP item I.

 B Telling Time

1. What time is it now?

2. What time will it be five minutes from now?

3. What time was it five minutes ago?

4. What time will it be one hour from now?

To show the indicated times, students may use a demonstration clock, draw clocks, or use the clocks they made in Unit 6 Lesson 1.

Student Questions	Teacher Notes

 Skinnies and Bits

Katie placed a bunch of base-ten pieces on her desk. She had 17 bits and 3 skinnies.

A. How many bits are the three skinnies made up of?

B. What number do all of Katie's pieces represent?

C. What other pieces could Katie have used to represent this same number?

A. 30

B. 47

C. Answers may vary. One possible answer is 4 skinnies and 7 bits.

Skip Counting by Fives and Tens

1. Skip count by tens to 150, starting at 50.

2. Skip count by fives to 100, starting at 40.

3. Alex, Renee, Dana, Leroy, and Kenya combined their marbles. Alex had 50 marbles. Renee had 10 marbles. Dana had 10, Leroy had 5, and Kenya had 3 marbles. How many marbles do they have in all?

In Lesson 3 students use mass sets to balance objects on an equal-arm balance. For example, the mass of an eraser might equal the mass of three 10-gram masses, one 5-gram mass, and two 1-gram masses. Practice in skip counting by fives and tens will help students determine the total mass of the objects.

1. 50, 60, 70 . . . 130, 140, 150

2. 40, 45, 50 . . . 90, 95, 100

3. 78 marbles

An Added Plus

| | | $\begin{array}{r}7\\+3\end{array}$ |

A. $9 + 1 =$ ___

B. $10 + 2 =$ ___

C. ___ $= 3 + 10$

D. ___ $= 9 + 2$

E. $3 + 9 =$ ___

F. $9 + 4 =$ ___

G. $4 + 10 =$ ___

H. ___ $= 10 + 1$

A. 10
B. 12
C. 13
D. 11
E. 12
F. 13
G. 14
H. 11

 Base-Ten Board

N

What number is each student representing?

1. Marge placed 4 flats and 2 skinnies on the *Base-Ten Board.*

2. John placed 2 flats, 3 skinnies, and 14 bits on the board.

3. Patty placed 3 flats and 20 skinnies on the board.

1. 420
2. 244
3. 500

Use a transparency of the *Base-Ten Board* from Unit 6 Lesson 3. Place the pieces on the board for each problem. Ask student volunteers to represent each number a different way.

Student Questions	Teacher Notes

 Practice with Money

A. Tom had 4 nickels. Sam had 10 pennies. How many coins do the two boys have altogether?

B. How much are the coins worth?

C. Jack found 9 nickels in his coat pocket and 3 nickels on his desk. How many nickels did Jack find in all?

D. How much are Jack's nickels worth?

A. 14 coins

B. 30 cents

C. 12 nickels

D. 60 cents

H **Which Is Which?**

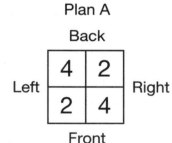

Plan A
Back

4	2
2	4

Left ⎸ ⎸ Right

Front

Plan B
Back

4	4
2	2

Left ⎸ ⎸ Right

Front

1. Which cube model belongs to Plan A?

2. Which cube model belongs to Plan B?

3. What is the volume of each cube model?

4. What is the height of each?

Build two cube models according to the plans. Display the models and the cube model plans. When you display the models, make sure that the front of each model faces the students. Students worked with cube models in Unit 6.

3. 12 cubic units; 12 cubic units

4. 4 units; 4 units

I Addition Facts Quiz: Group F

A. $3 + 9 =$ ___

B. $1 + 10 =$ ___

C. ___ $= 4 + 9$

D. $10 + 3 =$ ___

E. $1 + 9 =$ ___

F. ___ $= 10 + 4$

G. ___ $= 9 + 2$

H. $2 + 10 =$ ___

I. Explain your strategy for C.

A. 12

B. 11

C. 13

D. 13

E. 10

F. 14

G. 11

H. 12

I. Answers may vary. One possible strategy: add $10 + 4 = 14$, then subtract 1 (because 9 is 1 less than 10) to get 13.

J Ordering Masses

Enrique measured the mass of three different bags of marbles. He found that the blue bag had the most mass and that the red bag had more mass than the green bag. Order the three bags from the greatest mass to the least mass.

It may be helpful for students to write "blue," "green," and "red" on slips of paper. As you read the statement, students can move the slips of paper to model the order. Once students think they know the order, reread the statement while students check their answers.

blue, red, green

Student Questions	Teacher Notes

 What's the Difference?

A. 12 − 3 = ___

B. 14 − 10 = ___

C. ___ = 11 − 1

D. 13 − 4 = ___

E. ___ = 11 − 9

F. ___ = 12 − 2

G. 10 − 9 = ___

H. 13 − 3 = ___

Using the related addition fact is a strategy students may find helpful. Encourage students to develop and share their own strategies for the subtraction facts.

A. 9

B. 4

C. 10

D. 9

E. 2

F. 10

G. 1

H. 10

 Line 'Em Up

Drew found three rocks and used the equal-arm balance at school to compare their masses. He found that:

A. The shiny rock had more mass than the black rock.

B. The black rock had less mass than the smooth rock.

C. The smooth rock had more mass than the shiny rock.

List the three rocks in order from greatest to least mass.

It may be helpful for students to write "shiny," "black," and "smooth" on slips of paper. As you read the statements, students can move the slips of paper to model the order. Once students think they know the order, reread the statements while students check their answers.

smooth, shiny, black

Daily Practice and Problems

A. *Triangle Flash Cards: Group F*
  (URG p. 8)

With a partner, use your *Triangle Flash Cards* to practice addition facts. Separate the cards into three piles: those facts you know and can answer quickly, those facts that you can figure out with a strategy, and those that you need to learn. Discuss the strategies that you use with your partner.

B. Telling Time (URG p. 8)

1. What time is it now?

2. What time will it be five minutes from now?

3. What time was it five minutes ago?

4. What time will it be one hour from now?

C. Skinnies and Bits (URG p. 9)

Katie placed a bunch of base-ten pieces on her desk. She had 17 bits and 3 skinnies.

A. How many bits are the three skinnies made up of?

B. What number do all of Katie's pieces represent?

C. What other pieces could Katie have used to represent this same number?

D. Skip Counting by Fives and Tens (URG p. 9)

1. Skip count by tens to 150, starting at 50.

2. Skip count by fives to 100, starting at 40.

3. Alex, Renee, Dana, Leroy, and Kenya combined their marbles. Alex had 50 marbles. Renee had 10 marbles. Dana had 10, Leroy had 5, and Kenya had 3 marbles. How many marbles do they have in all?

Suggestions for using the DPPs are on page 18.

LESSON GUIDE

Putting Masses in Order

Estimated Class Sessions:
2

This activity introduces students to the equal-arm balance and develops the concept of mass. Students compare masses with an equal-arm balance and put them in order, from largest mass to smallest. By experimenting with the objects selected for this activity, students probe some basic questions about mass.

Key Content

- Zeroing the equal-arm balance.

- Comparing and ordering the mass of objects using an equal-arm balance.

- Exploring the idea that mass depends on the material as well as the size of an object.

Key Vocabulary

equal-arm balance
mass

Materials List

Print Materials for Students

		Math Facts and Daily Practice and Problems	Activity	Homework	Written Assessment
Student Book	Student Guide		*Comparing Masses* Page 194 and *Analyzing Masses* Pages 195–196	*Mass Hunt* Page 197 and *Triangle Flash Cards: Group F* Pages 201–202	*Analyzing the Masses of Two Blocks* Page 199
Teacher Resources	Facts Resource Guide ⊙	DPP Item 8A Use *Triangle Flash Cards: Group F* to practice the addition facts for this group.			
	Unit Resource Guide	DPP Item A–D Pages 8–9 ⊙			

⊙ *available on Teacher Resource CD*

All Transparency Masters, Blackline Masters, and Assessment Blackline Masters in the Unit Resource Guide are on the Teacher Resource CD.

Supplies for Each Student

envelope for *Triangle Flash Cards*

Supplies for Each Student Pair

equal-arm balance
small piece of clay
1-inch wood sphere
1-inch glass sphere
$\frac{1}{2}$-inch steel sphere
connecting cube

Materials for the Teacher

Comparing the Masses of Two Blocks Transparency Master (Unit Resource Guide) Page 20
Observational Assessment Record (Unit Resource Guide, Pages 5–6 and Teacher Resource CD)
equal-arm balance
small piece of clay
1-inch wood sphere
1-inch glass sphere
$\frac{1}{2}$-inch steel sphere
connecting cube
Note: This activity is based on the manipulatives listed above. If you use other objects, the questions on the activity pages will need to be modified.

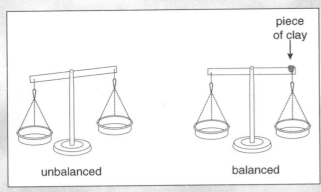

piece
of clay

unbalanced   balanced

Figure 1: *Using clay to zero the equal-arm balance*

Content Note

The **equal-arm balance** is a measurement tool used to compare the mass of objects. When an object is placed in each pan, the pan containing more mass moves down. If two masses are equal, the pans balance, and the arm of the balance comes to rest in a horizontal position. To work correctly, the balance arm should be horizontal when both pans are empty.

Name _____   Date _____

Comparing Masses

Draw

Predict and line up objects from most mass to least mass. Draw and label the order of your objects.

Compare masses on the equal-arm balance. Record your results in the table.

Mass Comparison Data Table

Object in Pan 1	Object in Pan 2	More Mass

194 **SG · Grade 2 · Unit 8 · Lesson 1**   **Putting Masses in Order**

Student Guide **- Page 194**

Before the Activity

Make sure you allow enough time to assemble the equal-arm balances if necessary. It is preferable to have students zero the equal-arm balance themselves to build understanding of how this measurement tool works. Allow time for students to explore the equal-arm balances before beginning the lesson.

Developing the Activity

Demonstrate how to zero the equal-arm balance. Stick a small piece of clay on the high end of the arm to bring it in line as shown in Figure 1. Have students work in pairs to zero their equal-arm balances. Through trial and error, students will find the proper amount of clay needed.

After introducing the equal-arm balance as a measurement tool, show the students the following objects: a one-inch wood sphere, a one-inch glass sphere, a half-inch steel sphere, and a connecting cube. Ask students to predict which object is heaviest, which is second heaviest, and so on. Have them explain their reasoning. Pay attention to whether students predict that larger objects are heavier. Now pass out one set of objects to each student team and ask them to line up their objects on their desks in the order they think is most mass to least mass. Students can compare the objects by holding one in each hand.

TIMS Tip

To line up the objects according to predicted mass, students can place them between two parallel rulers to prevent the spheres from rolling away.

Students should illustrate their predicted mass order on the *Comparing Masses* Activity Page. A sample drawing is shown in Figure 2.

Figure 2: *A picture showing the predicted mass order of four objects*

Have students use the equal-arm balance to verify their predictions. They will compare these four objects, two at a time, to determine which has the most mass. Students should keep track of their comparisons on the Mass Comparison Data Table. If there is a change from the predicted order, they can reposition one of the objects to show the proper order. For example, if students order their objects as steel sphere, glass sphere, wood sphere, and connecting cube and find that the connecting cube has more mass than the wood sphere, then they reorder the objects on their desks accordingly. Students' strategies for working through this part of the activity will vary. Some students may find that recording each comparison on the Mass Comparison Data Table is useful. Other students may be able to work directly moving the objects after comparing with the equal-arm balance until the objects are arranged correctly.

Ask students to record the order from most mass to least mass in the Mass Order Data Table on the *Analyzing Masses* Activity Pages. Students should work with a partner to discuss and respond to the questions that follow the data table. The questions guide students to use their experiences to draw valid conclusions and form generalizations. For example, two objects of the same size and shape but composed of different materials do not always have the same mass. It is not possible to determine the correct answers to **Questions 6** and **7** because we do not know the material that makes up the objects that are illustrated. You may explain the rationale for choosing the objects in this activity:

- Through direct experiences with these objects, we see that a larger size object does not always have more mass.

- The wood sphere and the glass sphere are the same size and shape, but their masses are different.

- The steel sphere is smaller than the other two spheres, but it has a larger mass than the wood sphere.

Conclude the lesson with a class discussion using *Comparing the Masses of Two Blocks* Transparency Master. Ask students to discuss the following question with their partners: Does Block A have more mass than Block B? This question is similar to **Questions 6** and **7** from the *Analyzing Masses* Activity Pages. Invite students to share their responses with the class. Record some of their responses on the transparency to show ways of explaining why the question cannot be answered. For example, *We cannot compare the masses unless we know the materials used to make the blocks.*

Name _____ Date _____

Analyzing Masses

Decide on the order of masses, and fill in the table below.

Mass Order Data Table

Mass Order	Name of Object
Most Mass	
Least Mass	

1. Which objects are the same size and shape?
   _____

2. Do these two objects have the same mass? Why?
   _____

3. Are the wood and steel spheres the same shape?
   _____

4. Which is smaller: the wood or steel sphere? _____

Putting Masses in Order   SG · Grade 2 · Unit 8 · Lesson 1 195

Student Guide - Page 195

Name _____ Date _____

5. Which has more mass: the wood or steel sphere? _____

6. Two new spheres are shown below. Which has more mass? Explain.

   A   B
   _____
   _____
   _____

7. Cylinder A and Cylinder B are the same shape and size.

   A   B

Mark the correct statement below.

_____ The masses are the same.

_____ Cylinder B has more mass.

_____ Cylinder A has more mass.

_____ You can't tell which has more mass.

196 SG · Grade 2 · Unit 8 · Lesson 1   Putting Masses in Order

Student Guide - Page 196

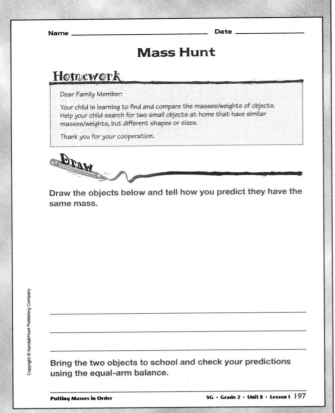

Student Guide - Page 197

Suggestions for Teaching the Lesson

Math Facts

DPP item A reminds students to practice the addition facts in Group F using their *Triangle Flash Cards*.

Homework and Practice

- The *Mass Hunt* Homework Page asks students to search for two objects at home that they predict have the same mass. Remind students to bring the objects to school so that they can check their predictions using the equal-arm balances.

- DPP item B involves telling time. Item C develops understanding of place value using base-ten pieces. Item D provides practice skip counting which will help prepare students for the laboratory investigation in Lesson 3.

- Assign the *Triangle Flash Cards: Group F* in the *Student Guide* as ongoing homework. Discuss possible strategies for learning these facts. Using tens, making tens, and counting on are effective strategies.

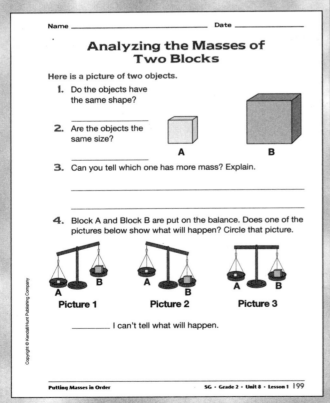

Student Guide - Page 199

Student Guide - Page 202

Assessment

- The *Analyzing the Masses of Two Blocks* Assessment Page asks students to judge the size, shape, and mass of two different-sized cubes. Students' responses provide a measure of their abilities to draw conclusions about mass and materials.

- Use the *Observational Assessment Record* to note students' abilities to compare the mass of objects using the equal-arm balance.

Extension

Each student pair can gather and show the class four different objects that will be difficult to order according to mass based on observation only. Students will try to predict the order of the objects from most mass to least mass. They then check their predictions with an equal-arm balance.

AT A GLANCE

Math Facts and Daily Practice and Problems (A5)

DPP item A provides practice with addition facts using *Triangle Flash Cards: Group F.* Item B involves time. Students develop place value understanding in item C and skip-counting skills in item D.

Developing the Activity (A1)

1. Students zero equal-arm balances.
2. Students predict the order of mass from greatest to least for four objects.
3. Students record their predictions on the *Comparing Masses* Activity Page.
4. Students compare objects' masses using equal-arm balances.
5. Students record the correct order and answer questions on the *Analyzing Masses* Activity Pages.
6. Students discuss the effects of size and material on mass with the *Comparing the Masses of Two Blocks* Transparency Master.

Homework

1. Students complete the *Mass Hunt* Homework Page.
2. Send *Triangle Flash Cards: Group F* home with students to study with family members.

Assessment

1. Students complete the *Analyzing the Masses of Two Blocks* Assessment Page.
2. Use Assessment Indicator (A1) and the *Observational Assessment Record* to note students' abilities to compare the mass of objects.

Notes:

Comparing the Masses of Two Blocks

Does Block A have more mass than Block B? Explain.

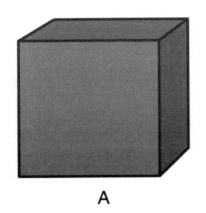

A

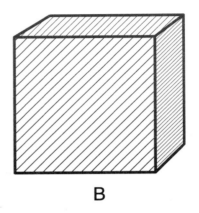

B

_____

_____

_____

_____

_____

Student Guide

Comparing Masses (SG p. 194)

*See Figure 2 in Lesson Guide 1 for a sample drawing.
Mass comparisons will vary.

Analyzing Masses (SG pp. 195–196)

Questions 1–7

The order of the objects from most mass to least
mass is: steel sphere, glass sphere, wood sphere,
connecting cube.

1. The glass sphere and the wood sphere
2. No. They are made of different materials.
3. Yes.
4. The steel sphere
5. The steel sphere
6. *Impossible to tell
7. *You can't tell which has more mass.

Mass Hunt (SG p. 197)

Answers will vary.

Analyzing the Masses of Two Blocks (SG p. 199)

Questions 1–4

1. Yes.
2. No.
3. *No, we need to know the material used to make the blocks.
4. *You can't tell what will happen.

Unit Resource Guide

Comparing the Masses of Two Blocks (URG p. 20)

You can't tell. You need to put them on a balance.

*Answers and/or discussion are included in the Lesson Guide.

Daily Practice and Problems

E. An Added Plus (URG p. 10)

A. $9 + 1 = $ ___

B. $10 + 2 = $ ___

C. ___ $= 3 + 10$

D. ___ $= 9 + 2$

E. $3 + 9 = $ ___

F. $9 + 4 = $ ___

G. $4 + 10 = $ ___

H. ___ $= 10 + 1$

F. Base-Ten Board (URG p. 10)

What number is each student representing?

1. Marge placed 4 flats and 2 skinnies on the *Base-Ten Board*.

2. John placed 2 flats, 3 skinnies, and 14 bits on the board.

3. Patty placed 3 flats and 20 skinnies on the board.

Suggestions for using the DPPs are on page 30.

LESSON GUIDE 2

The Mouse-Proof Shelf

Estimated Class Sessions: 1

In their quest for cheese, four mice named Millie, Minnie, Marty, and Mike must surmount an obstacle—a lamp suspended by a cord. The lamp dangles beneath the shelf where the cheese is kept. To keep the lamp from tilting, one mouse jumps on either side. This plan fails because the mass of each mouse is different. The mice turn their failure into a success, however, by applying what they have learned about mass. They jump in pairs to balance the lamp, climb the cord to reach the shelf, and then snack on the cheese.

Key Content

- Applying the concept of balancing masses.
- Solving a multiple-solution problem.
- Solving computation problems involving mass.
- Connecting mathematics and science to language arts: reading a story involving mass.

Materials List

Print Materials for Students

	Math Facts and Daily Practice and Problems	Activity
Student Guide		*Millie, Minnie, Marty, and Mike Did It!* Pages 203–204
Adventure Book		*The Mouse-Proof Shelf* Pages 31–44
Facts Resource Guide 🔘	DPP Item 8E	
Unit Resource Guide 🔘	DPP Items E–F Page 10	

(Student Books: Student Guide, Adventure Book; Teacher Resources: Facts Resource Guide, Unit Resource Guide)

🔘 *available on Teacher Resource CD*

All Transparency Masters, Blackline Masters, and Assessment Blackline Masters in the Unit Resource Guide are on the Teacher Resource CD.

Supplies for Each Student Pair

55 connecting cubes
equal-arm balance

Materials for the Teacher

Observational Assessment Record (Unit Resource Guide, Pages 5–6 and Teacher Resource CD)

Before the Activity

Before beginning the story, use the first page to introduce the four main characters. Write on the board the names of the four mice and the patterns on their shirts:

Millie – striped

Minnie – plain

Marty – zigzag

Mike – long dots

This list will make it easier for the students to keep the characters straight as you read the story.

Developing the Activity

Have students follow along in their Adventure Books as you read *The Mouse-Proof Shelf* aloud. Then, reread the story, pausing at the Discussion Prompts to check comprehension.

Discussion Prompts

Page 33

- *How is the lamp similar to an equal-arm balance?*

Both the lamp and the horizontal stick of an equal-arm balance tilt and can be used to compare mass.

Page 35

- *Compare Minnie's mass to Millie's mass based on what happens when they jump on the lamp.*

Millie has more mass than Minnie.

Adventure Book - Page 33

Adventure Book - Page 35

Adventure Book - Page 36

Page 36

- *Do you think Millie's plan to switch sides is a good idea? Use what you know about their masses to explain your answer.*

Millie's plan will not succeed. The lamp will still tilt because the mice's masses are different.

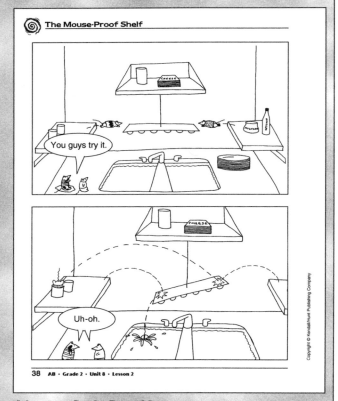

Adventure Book - Page 38

Page 38

- *Compare Marty's mass to Mike's mass based on what happens when they jump on the lamp.*

Marty has more mass than Mike.

Discussion Prompts

Page 41

- *Why do the mice know that Minnie's mass is greater than Marty's?*

The lamp tilts down on Minnie's side and spills her into the sink.

Adventure Book - Page 41

Page 42

- *Can you order the masses of the mice?*

Millie, Minnie, Marty, and Mike.

- *Why did the mice choose Millie and Mike for one team and Minnie and Marty for the other team?*
- *Why did they think those two teams would balance each other?*

Millie, who has the most mass, is coupled with Mike, who has the least mass. This pair may balance the team of Minnie and Marty, since they are ranked second and third, respectively, in mass order.

Adventure Book - Page 42

Discussion Prompts

- *Work with a partner to complete the* Millie, Minnie, Marty, and Mike Did It! *Activity Pages. How many combinations can you find for Millie and Mike to balance Minnie and Marty on the lamp?*

After discussing the story, student pairs should complete the *Millie, Minnie, Marty, and Mike Did It!* Activity Pages. Student pairs will need your guidance to help them get started. The problem presented has multiple answers: *How many different combinations of masses can you find for Millie and Mike to balance Minnie and Marty on the lamp?* Encourage students to find as many solutions as they can. Then, post and discuss students' solutions. Note that the masses of the mice are not realistic. It would be very difficult to find a 1-gram mouse! See Figure 3 for the 34 possible solutions.

Name _____ Date _____

Millie, Minnie, Marty, and Mike Did It!

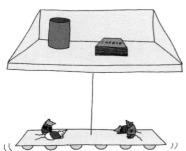

There are many possible combinations of masses for Millie and Mike, balancing Minnie and Marty on the hanging lamp. How many different combinations can you find?

Work with a partner. Pretend the mice can have any of these masses: 9 grams, 8 grams, 7 grams, 6 grams, 5 grams, 4 grams, 3 grams, 2 grams, or 1 gram. Each mouse has a different mass.

You can use connecting cubes to represent each mouse's mass to check your combinations on the equal-arm balance.

Record the combinations of masses in the tables on the next page.

The Mouse–Proof Shelf   SG · Grade 2 · Unit 8 · Lesson 2 203

Student Guide - Page 203

Name _____ Date _____

Millie's and Mike's total mass should equal Minnie's and Marty's total mass. The first row shows an example.

Mouse Masses in Grams

Millie	Mike	Total	Minnie	Marty	Total
8	1	9	5	4	9

204 SG · Grade 2 · Unit 8 · Lesson 2   The Mouse–Proof Shelf

Student Guide - Page 204

Mouse Masses in Grams

Millie + Mike	Minnie + Marty		Millie + Mike	Minnie + Marty
9 + 6	8 + 7		6 + 1	5 + 2
9 + 5	8 + 6		5 + 2	4 + 3
9 + 4	8 + 5		5 + 1	4 + 2
9 + 3	8 + 4		4 + 1	3 + 2
9 + 2	8 + 3		9 + 4	7 + 6
9 + 1	8 + 2		9 + 3	7 + 5
8 + 5	7 + 6		9 + 2	7 + 4
8 + 4	7 + 5		9 + 1	7 + 3
8 + 3	7 + 4		8 + 3	6 + 5
8 + 2	7 + 3		8 + 2	6 + 4
8 + 1	7 + 2		8 + 1	6 + 3
7 + 4	6 + 5		7 + 2	5 + 4
7 + 3	6 + 4		7 + 1	5 + 3
7 + 2	6 + 3		6 + 1	4 + 3
7 + 1	6 + 2		9 + 2	6 + 5
6 + 3	5 + 4		9 + 1	6 + 4
6 + 2	5 + 3		8 + 1	5 + 4

Figure 3: *Thirty-four Possible Solutions for the* Millie, Minnie, Marty, and Mike Did It! *Activity Pages*

Suggestions for Teaching the Lesson

Math Facts

- DPP item E provides practice with the addition facts in Group F.
- Students practice math facts as they solve the problem on the *Millie, Minnie, Marty, and Mike Did It!* Activity Pages in the *Student Guide*.

Homework and Practice

- DPP item F builds understanding of place value using base-ten pieces.
- Remind students to practice the addition facts in Group F using their *Triangle Flash Cards*.

Assessment

Use the *Observational Assessment Record* to note students' progress comparing the mass of objects using the equal-arm balance.

Answer Key • Lesson 2: The Mouse-Proof Shelf

Student Guide

Millie, Minnie, Marty, and Mike Did It!
(SG p. 204)

*See Figure 3 for a complete list of possible solutions.

*Answers and/or discussion are included in the Lesson Guide.

LESSON GUIDE ③

Measuring Mass

Estimated
Class
Sessions:
3

Measuring Mass is a laboratory investigation in which students measure the mass of objects in grams. They use an equal-arm balance and standard metric masses to find the number of grams in some everyday objects. The idea that material is an important variable in determining mass is reinforced.

Key Content

• Measuring the mass of objects in grams using an equal-arm balance and standard masses.

• Solving computation problems involving mass.

• Collecting and organizing data.

• Making and interpreting a bar graph.

• Connecting mathematics and science to real-world situations: measuring mass.

Key Vocabulary

gram

Daily Practice and Problems

G. Practice with Money (URG p. 11) $

A. Tom had 4 nickels. Sam had 10 pennies. How many coins do the two boys have altogether?

B. How much are the coins worth?

C. Jack found 9 nickels in his coat pocket and 3 nickels on his desk. How many nickels did Jack find in all?

D. How much are Jack's nickels worth?

H. Which Is Which? (URG p. 11)

```
       Plan A                    Plan B
       Back                      Back
     ┌───┬───┐                 ┌───┬───┐
Left │ 4 │ 2 │ Right      Left │ 4 │ 4 │ Right
     ├───┼───┤                 ├───┼───┤
     │ 2 │ 4 │                 │ 2 │ 2 │
     └───┴───┘                 └───┴───┘
       Front                     Front
```

1. Which cube model belongs to Plan A?

2. Which cube model belongs to Plan B?

3. What is the volume of each cube model?

4. What is the height of each?

I. Addition Facts Quiz: Group F
(URG p. 12)

A. $3 + 9 = $ __

B. $1 + 10 = $ __

C. __ $ = 4 + 9$

D. $10 + 3 = $ __

E. $1 + 9 = $ __

F. __ $ = 10 + 4$

G. __ $ = 9 + 2$

H. $2 + 10 = $ __

I. Explain your strategy for C.

J. Ordering Masses (URG p. 12)

Enrique measured the mass of three different bags of marbles. He found that the blue bag had the most mass and that the red bag had more mass than the green bag. Order the three bags from the greatest mass to the least mass.

K. What's the Difference? (URG p. 13)

A. $12 - 3 = $ __

B. $14 - 10 = $ __

C. __ $ = 11 - 1$

D. $13 - 4 = $ __

E. __ $ = 11 - 9$

F. __ $ = 12 - 2$

G. $10 - 9 = $ __

H. $13 - 3 = $ __

L. Line 'Em Up (URG p. 13)

Drew found three rocks and used the equal-arm balance at school to compare their masses. He found that:

A. The shiny rock had more mass than the black rock.

B. The black rock had less mass than the smooth rock.

C. The smooth rock had more mass than the shiny rock.

List the three rocks in order from greatest to least mass.

Suggestions for using the DPPs are on pages 36–37.

Materials List

Print Materials for Students

		Math Facts and Daily Practice and Problems	Lab	Homework	Written Assessment
Student Book	**Student Guide**		*Measuring Mass* Pages 205–209	*What's the Total Mass?* Page 211	
Teacher Resources	**Facts Resource Guide**	DPP Items 8G, 8H, 8*I* & 8K			DPP Item 8*I* *Addition Facts Quiz: Group F*
	Unit Resource Guide	DPP Items G–L Pages 11–13	*Gram E Award* Page 40, 1 teacher-prepared award per contestant (optional) and *Rock E Road* Page 41, 1 per student (optional)		DPP Item I *Addition Facts Quiz: Group F* Page 12
	Generic Section		*Vertical Bar Graph*, 1 per student		

⊙ available on Teacher Resource CD

All Transparency Masters, Blackline Masters, and Assessment Blackline Masters in the Unit Resource Guide are on the Teacher Resource CD.

Supplies for Each Student Pair

set of standard metric masses
equal-arm balance (zeroed in the first activity)
10–15 small classroom objects, each having a mass less than 100 grams
4 or 5 objects of approximately 100 grams each

Materials for the Teacher

Transparency of Measuring Mass Data Table (Student Guide) Page 206
Transparency of *Vertical Bar Graph* (Unit Resource Guide, Generic Section), optional
Observational Assessment Record (Unit Resource Guide, Pages 5–6 and Teacher Resource CD)
Individual Assessment Record Sheet (Teacher Implementation Guide, Assessment section and
    Teacher Resource CD)
set of standard metric masses
equal-arm balance (zeroed in the first activity)
4 small classroom objects less than 100 grams
object of approximately 100 grams

Object	Mass (in g)	Object	Mass (in g)
eraser	38 g	shoe (Size 8.5 adult)	334 g
chalk (1 piece)	11 g	sandwich	100 g
#2 pencil (19 cm, 0.7 d)	5 g	medium apple	150 g
5 connecting links	6.8 g	250 cc graduated cylinder	82 g
small scissors	19 g	100 cc graduated cylinder	35 g
12" plastic ruler	16 g	150 cc beaker	97 g
meterstick	109 g		

Figure 4: *Masses of some classroom objects*

Before the Lab

Display a wide variety of objects for children to use in the lab. Each student pair will find the mass of four objects that have masses less than 100 grams and one that has a mass greater than 100 grams. Student pairs may share the objects. Refer to the classroom items listed in Figure 4 for ideas.

Developing the Lab

Part 1. Demonstrating the Lab and Drawing the Picture

Explain that in this lab, students will find the mass of several classroom objects. To help them understand the process, demonstrate how they will use the equal-arm balance. Put one of the light objects in one pan, and place the standard masses in the other pan until the balance is level. During your demonstration, emphasize the different sizes of standard masses: 1 gram, 5 grams, 10 grams, and 20 grams. The **gram** is the basic unit used to measure mass. As you level the balance, make sure students know which standard masses you are using and how many of each. Ask students to share their observations. Ask questions such as:

- *I place two 5-gram masses and two 1-gram masses in the pan. What is the total mass in the pan?*

- *Which has more mass—the standard masses or the object? How can you tell?*

- *Should I place more grams in the pan or should I take some out? Why do you think so?*

- *Which piece(s) should I remove from the pan? Which piece(s) should I place in the pan?*

- *Is it balanced? What is the total mass of the object? How did you figure it out?*

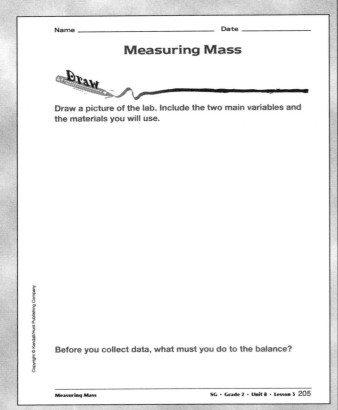

Student Guide - Page 205

The Student Guide page 205 contains:

Name _____ Date _____

Measuring Mass

Draw

Draw a picture of the lab. Include the two main variables and the materials you will use.

Before you collect data, what must you do to the balance?

Measuring Mass   SG · Grade 2 · Unit 8 · Lesson 3   205

Student Guide - Page 206

The Student Guide page 206 contains:

Name _____ Date _____

Collect

Find any object that is approximately 100 grams and 4 small objects to mass. Both partners should find the mass of each object on their own and then check each other's results.

Measuring Mass Data Table

N Name of Object	1 Gram	5 Grams	10 Grams	20 Grams	M Total Mass (in ____ unit)

Graph

Make a bar graph of the data. Label both axes.

206 SG · Grade 2 · Unit 8 · Lesson 3   Measuring Mass

Discuss the two main variables—Name of object *(N)* and Mass *(M)*. Ask each child to draw a picture of the investigation on the *Measuring Mass* Lab Pages using your demonstration as a guide. The pictures should communicate the important elements of the investigation as well as the two main variables. The pictures might include some of the objects the students would like to measure, the equal-arm balances, and the standard masses. Including items such as these will make the procedure of the lab apparent as you examine the picture. See Figure 5 for a sample student picture.

Figure 5: *A picture communicating key elements in the lab*

Part 2. Collecting and Graphing the Data

Before students begin to collect data, have them check the equal-arm balances to make sure they are still zeroed from the first activity. Then, display a transparency of the data table on the *Measuring Mass* Lab Pages on the overhead projector. Find the mass of two or three objects with the class. Discuss how to record the number of each of the standard masses used and the total mass of each object.

After balancing an object, display the gram masses and find the total mass with the class. For example, display one 20-gram, two 10-grams, one 5-gram, and three 1-grams. Have students share different ways of finding the total mass. Starting on 20, a student may count 30, 40, 45, 46, 47, 48. The *200 Chart* or other tools may be helpful to some students as they add up the masses.

Ask student pairs to choose at least five objects— one object that is approximately 100 grams and four objects that are less than 100 grams. They can measure more than one of an identical object (e.g., 3 unused pieces of chalk) but should indicate this on the data table. Tell students that they may find the mass of any object that interests them as long as it fits in the pan. However, point out that objects with a large mass may not be recorded on the bar graph. (The scale chosen for the *Vertical Bar Graph* will determine if all the masses for all the objects will fit

Measuring Mass Data Table

N Name of Object	1 Gram	5 Grams	10 Grams	20 Grams	M Mass (in grams/unit)
eraser	3	1	3		38 g
12 in plastic ruler	1	1	1		16 g
meterstick	4	1		5	109 g
150 cc graduated cylinder	1		1	2	51 g
3 pieces of chalk	3	2	2		33 g

Figure 6: *A sample data table*

on the bar graph.) Ask students to keep the objects available for checking. Partners should find the mass of the same object, making sure the pans balance. Each student should independently count the masses, and determine the total mass *(M)*. Then, if there is a discrepancy, they can double-check their work and reach agreement on the mass of each object before recording it on the Measuring Mass Data Table.

After the data collection is complete, students are ready to make a graph. The sample data shown in Figure 6 ranges from 16 grams to 109 grams, which means students need a scale on the vertical axis exceeding 100 grams. Skip counting by fives works best for the sample data in Figure 6. It may be helpful to guide students by showing a transparency of the *Vertical Bar Graph*. With your assistance, pairs of students should make their own decisions about how to scale their graphs. Remind students to put the units of mass on the vertical scale and to label both axes with the appropriate symbols. Then, they will need to use number sense to place the mass values on the graph.

TIMS Tip
The balance may not be perfectly level if the true mass of the object is, for example, $16\frac{1}{2}$ grams. With 16 grams in one pan, the balance will tilt toward the object. With 17 grams, it will tilt toward the mass side. Children may figure out that the true mass is between 16 and 17 grams, and therefore $16\frac{1}{2}$ grams may be a better number to record.

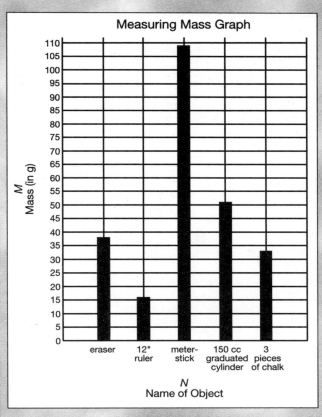

Figure 7: *A student's graph*

Part 3. Analyzing the Data

Have student pairs complete the Explore questions on the *Measuring Mass* Lab Pages in the *Student Guide.* Students use their graphs or data tables to obtain the information needed to solve these multistep problems. *Question 3* specifically focuses on the additive property of mass. Students may possibly find a difference of a gram or so because both objects could have been a bit over or under the whole number mass and would not show on the balance until the error is compounded.

> ### 📓 Journal Prompt
> Show students a small, unopened spice jar with the mass (in grams) of the contents printed on the label. Pose this problem to the children: *How can you find the mass of the container without opening the jar? Think about how you can solve this problem.* Have students write their problem-solving strategies in their journals.

Suggestions for Teaching the Lesson

Math Facts

DPP item G provides practice with addition math facts and with calculating money. For item H students use math facts to solve a cube model problem. Item K provides practice with the subtraction facts related to Group F.

Homework and Practice

- The *What's the Total Mass?* Homework Page uses the context of finding the total mass of an object to provide practice solving addition problems with multiple addends. As you discuss the homework, encourage students to share their problem-solving strategies.

- DPP items J and L are word problems that provide practice ordering objects according to their mass.

Assessment

- Observe students as they measure the mass of the objects. Document their skills using the *Observational Assessment Record.*

- Use students' completed lab pages and graphs to measure their abilities to solve problems involving mass and to make and interpret bar graphs. Use the following criteria to assess the graphs: (1) the axes are labeled with appropriate symbols, (2) the vertical axis is scaled properly, and (3) the values for the objects are carefully plotted. Record students' progress on the *Observational Assessment Record.*

Student Guide content (Page 207)

Name _____ Date _____

Explore

1. **A.** Which of your objects has the least mass?

   B. If you had four of these objects, would their combined mass be more than 100 grams or less than 100 grams?

   How did you figure it out?

2. **A.** Which of your objects has the most mass?

   B. Would three 40-gram objects have more mass or less mass than your heaviest object?

   How did you figure it out?

Measuring Mass   SG · Grade 2 · Unit 8 · Lesson 3   207

Student Guide - Page 207

Student Guide content (Page 208)

Name _____ Date _____

3. **A.** Find the sum of the masses of your heaviest object and your lightest object.

   B. Put these two objects in one balance pan and find their total mass. Did you get the same answer as in Question 3A? Why or why not?

4.

   | 1 | heaviest object | ____ | lightest objects

   How many of your lighter objects come closest to balancing your heaviest object? How do you know?

208   SG · Grade 2 · Unit 8 · Lesson 3   Measuring Mass

Student Guide - Page 208

- Use students' journal entries to assess their abilities to devise an effective strategy for determining the mass of a container without opening the jar. Have them create a plan in their journals. They can find the mass of a jar with the spice and then subtract the mass of the spice from the total. Or they can put the spice jar in one pan and then put masses to equal the contents from the label in the second pan. They then count as masses are added to make the pans balanced.

- Use DPP item I to assess students' progress with the addition math facts in Group F. Making tens, using tens, and counting on are appropriate strategies for these facts. Document students' progress on the *Observational Assessment Record*.

- Transfer appropriate documentation from the Unit 8 *Observational Assessment Record* to students' *Individual Assessment Record Sheets*.

Extension

- Ask students to find two objects—one rock and another object—that they estimate to be close to 50 grams. These items may be found at home or in school. Have students check the accuracy of their estimations by using the equal-arm balances and standard masses. Create two separate class charts or data tables—one for the rock data and one for the other objects that were collected. Ask students to record their names, their objects, and the appropriate masses on the class chart. After everyone's data has been recorded, ask:

  - *Which objects are close to 50 grams?*
  - *Which rocks are close to 50 grams?*

  Invite the class to help decide a range that would qualify an object or rock as being close to 50 grams. You can use a range of 40–60 grams.

- Direct students' attention to those objects which are close to 50 grams. Ask questions such as:

  - *Which object is the largest in size?*
  - *Which rock is the smallest in size?*

  Through a class discussion, guide students to restate the key ideas about mass presented in this unit. For example, students might say, *"A small object can have more mass than a big one,"* or *"Because a rock is big, it doesn't mean that it has more mass."* If by chance, any of the rocks have the same mass, you will want to take time to compare them. Ask questions such as:

  - *Are the rocks the same shape?*
  - *Do they appear to be the same size?*
  - *Are they made of the same material?*

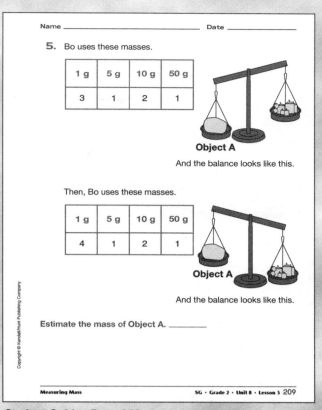

Student Guide - Page 209

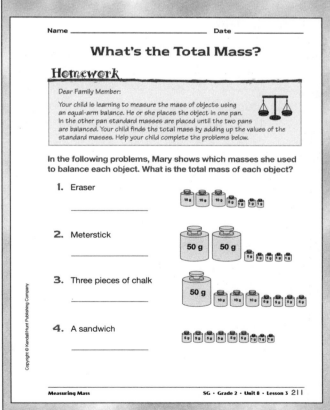

Student Guide - Page 211

- Present the *Gram E Award* to every student who entered an object and a rock in the contest. Then, to conclude this activity, ask students to complete the *Rock E Road* Blackline Master. Students can use counters to help them solve the problems.

AT A GLANCE

Math Facts and Daily Practice and Problems (A5)

DPP item G practices math facts and calculating money. Item H is a problem using cube models. Item I assesses the addition facts in Group F. Items J and L involve ordering objects according to their mass. Item K practices subtraction facts related to Group F.

Part 1. Demonstrating the Lab and Drawing the Picture

1. Demonstrate how to balance an object using an equal-arm balance and standard masses.
2. Introduce the two main variables—*N*, Name of Object, and *M*, Mass.
3. Students draw a picture of the investigation on the *Measuring Mass* Lab Pages.

Part 2. Collecting and Graphing the Data (A2) (A3) (A4)

1. Students check that their equal-arm balances are zeroed.
2. Balance two or three objects with the class and discuss how to find the total mass.
3. Demonstrate how to record the data on a transparency of the data table on the *Measuring Mass* Lab Pages in the *Student Guide*.
4. Student pairs choose at least five objects—one object that is approximately 100 grams and four objects that are less than 100 grams.
5. Students balance each object and individuals determine the total mass.
6. Students compare their results with a partner and then record the data for each object on the Measuring Mass Data Table.
7. Using a transparency of the *Vertical Bar Graph,* assist students in scaling their graphs and labeling axes.
8. Students graph their data on the *Vertical Bar Graph.*

Part 3. Analyzing the Data (A4)

Students complete the Explore *Questions 1–5* on the *Measuring Mass* Lab Pages.

Homework

Students complete the *What's the Total Mass?* Homework Page.

AT A GLANCE

Assessment

1. Use Assessment Indicators (A2, A3, A4) and the *Observational Assessment Record* to document students' abilities to measure mass in grams, make and interpret bar graphs, and solve problems involving mass.

2. Use DPP item I, Assessment Indicator (A5), and the *Observational Assessment Record* to document students' progress with the math facts in Group F.

3. Transfer appropriate documentation from the Unit 8 *Observational Assessment Record* to students' *Individual Assessment Record Sheets*.

Extension (A2) (A4) (Optional)

1. Students find one rock and another object they predict to be close to 50 grams.

2. Students use the equal-arm balance and standard masses to check their predictions.

3. Students record the masses of their two objects on class charts or data tables.

4. As a class, decide on a range that would qualify an object or rock as being close to 50 grams.

5. Of those that qualify, discuss which is the largest and which is the smallest in size.

6. Present the *Gram E Award* to students who participated.

7. Students complete the *Rock E Road* Activity Page.

Notes:

Gram E Award

This **Gram E Award** is awarded to _____
for outstanding work in searching for a 50-gram object and a
50-gram rock.

_____

Your teacher

Rock E Road

Set your own rock on the Rock E Road as you solve the problems. Connecting cubes or other counters might help you.

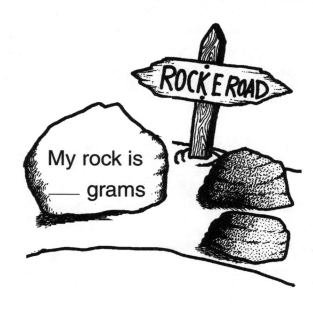

My rock is
____ grams

1. What if your rock had a mass twin? What would their total mass be?

   _____

2. What if your rock belonged to a set of mass triplets?

   What would their total mass be? _____

3. What if your rock was broken into four equal parts?

   What would the mass of each part be? _____

4. What if your rock needed to be cut into thirds? How

   much mass should each piece have? _____

5. What if your rock was smashed into tiny pebbles of 2 grams each? How many pebbles would there be?

   _____

Student Guide

Measuring Mass (SG pp. 207–209)

Questions 1–5

*See Figure 5 in Lesson Guide 3 for a sample picture. Students must zero the balance.

*See Figure 6 in Lesson Guide 3 for a sample table.

*See Figure 7 in Lesson Guide 3 for a sample graph.

  1.–4. Answers will vary.

  5. Object A is between 78 and 79 grams.

What's the Total Mass? (SG p. 211)

Questions 1–4

  1. 38 grams

  2. 109 grams

  3. 100 grams

  4. 33 grams

Unit Resource Guide

Rock E Road (URG p. 41)

Questions 1–5

  1.–5. Answers will vary.

*Answers and/or discussion are included in the Lesson Guide.